LORD, WHERE ARE YOU?

I'm hip-deep in Alligators

Prayer Reflections for Those In the Business Community

Merle G. Franke

C.S.S. Publishing Company

Lima, Ohio

W9-APC-488

Copyright © 1985 by
The C.S.S. Publishing Company, Inc.
Lima, Ohio

All rights reserved. No portion of this book may be reproduced or utilized in any form or by any means, electronic or mechanical including photocopying, without permission in writing from the publisher. Inquiries should be addressed to: The C.S.S. Publishing Company, Inc., 628 South Main Street, Lima, Ohio 45804.

5824/ISBN 0-89536-740-8 PRINTED IN U.S.A.

Table of Contents

3. Praise The Lord For Molehills!

4. Blessed Are They Who Push On Through The Fog

5. Lord, Will You Be There When I Hang It Up?

Foreword

Probably one of the first questions some readers will ask is why *I* am writing a book of prayer-reflections for the business community. I'm not primarily a businessman; I'm an ordained pastor. So what gives me the credentials to write such a collection?

For one thing, I have had business men and women as parishioners and as close friends for nearly all of my adult life. I have shared their anguish and hurts and frustrations as they have attempted to apply their faith to their workaday world. For these people have also been — primarily in most cases — faithful members of the Christian community as well as the business community. They know the pulls and the stresses between the two.

And the church has not done an adequate job of assisting people to use their faith effectively in their "real world" of work. My friend Bill Diehl, for many years with Bethlehem Steel, has often raised this fact in the consciousness of church leaders, particularly in his first published book "Christianity and the Real World."

As friend and pastor to many saints in the world of business, I have made it a point in the last few years to ask some of these people to discuss with me the problems that face them precisely because of their strong Christian faith. I was somewhat taken aback by the avalanche of concerns they expressed! Issue after issue poured forth from these people — people who wanted desperately to remain true to the basic tenets that spring from the Christian faith, but which often directly oppose practices common to the world of commerce and business.

If I was astonished by the concerns and conflicts, I was also humbled by the deep desire of these people — at least the ones I interviewed — to hold fast to their Christian faith. My strong appreciation to them and the thousands like them whom I do not know.

The subject matter of these prayer-reflections comes almost entirely from those business people I interviewed in preparation for this volume. They even gave me many of the titles used.

Now for the definition of these contents. What are they? Well, they're certainly not the kind of prayers we have all long been accustomed to. In a sense they are reflections — quick fleeting reflections that I imagine might flick across the mind of a business person at the beginning or end of a busy day. If these reflections can capture a mood or relate to a genuine feeling, then perhaps the reader can make of each one a brief prayer. That's the intent in any case.

If these prayer-reflections assist some people in the business community to gather strength for the day, or to finish the day not too weary, or even to know that others are sharing their concerns, this book will have well served its purpose.

— Merle G. Franke
Austin, Texas

Oh God
the
Sky
Is
Falling!

The Sky Is Falling!

Chicken Little was right
after all
the sky *is* falling

> I'm chicken big
> I can't face it God
> can't go into that damned meeting
> what will I tell them
> production falling
> sales falling
> profits falling

maybe I'll just say
the sky is falling

> hold up my sky God
> it's kinda shaky
> I don't know
> what's held it up this long
> you maybe
> I hope

keep my sky blue
for a while longer
I don't need any more hail

> I need time
> I need breathing space
> I need courage to face it all
>> I need you God
>> and blue steady skies
>> smiling at me

I Should Be Enjoying This Success . . .

Here I am at the top God
right where I wanted to be

    how come we're seldom satisfied
    we plan and yearn and work
    setting our sights high

I know *I* did
worked my tail off
aiming for the top of the mountain
and here I am

    how come I'm still restless, God?
    maybe even unhappy
      perish the thought

        I should be enjoying this success
          what is it God?
          some kind of executive disease?
          a success depression?
          what is it God?
        or *is* the chase more exciting
        than the prize?

it's rather funny God
I've never been so applauded
yet not quite happy
maybe I should return
to the ranks
down in the valley

do you enjoy
being God?

      if there are still more mountains
      for me to climb
      I think I need
      more of your strength next time

      so I can enjoy the view

I Need Some Rest

When can I retire God?
now I'm just tired
discouraged
aching inside and out

> I want to quit
> everything
> my only desire is rest
> the oblivion of sleep

> > when did I forget you?
> > what was it like
> > when you were with me
> > or when I was aware of it?

> my head wasn't heavy with nods
> my senses weren't numb
> from overwork

help me find my rest God
in you
waken me to my purpose
your purpose

> > renew me
> > with strength and meaning
> > help me to stay with you
> > as I strain and stretch
> > in the uphill battle

I really don't want to retire
I just need some rest

> > Oh God
> > be my rest
> > my beginning
> > my conclusion

You Got My Attention!

I was scared God
off to the hospital
in the dark of night
sirens wailing
almost as loudly
as I

        somehow God
        the business suddenly
        was less important
        and life was more

back home again
it was only a scare

only

a beautiful scare
a marvelous scare

        somehow, God,
        the business kept going
        without me for a week
        they didn't even
        have to call me
        should I feel bad?
        or good?

thanks for the scare God
you got my attention
now I hope
you can keep it
without the sirens

        I guess I had
        your attention
        all along

I Think I'm Paranoid

Why shouldn't I be
    with all those people
    after me

            but am I really
            paranoid?
            do I really believe
            they're out to get me?

and who are they
    my colleagues
    my employees
    my competitors
    my board of directors
    I don't know
I just have that feeling God
gnawing away at me
a jumpy stomach
a nervous laugh
        that's what happened to my friend
        and he was stronger than most
        stronger than I

            what was it I read
            the other night
            when I chanced upon a Psalm
            a rare Bible-reading night
            in a motel:

though a host should encamp
against me
I will not be afraid

            was the Psalmist paranoid too?
            I'm in good company -
            help me to laugh about it God

Why Do They Cheat?

I pay them well
I'm a good boss
they've got security
    but they cheat anyway

        I can't nail it down God
        but I know it
            expense accounts
            short hours
            sick leave
            you name it
            they've discovered it already

where has honesty gone God?
did I cheat
on the way up?
    why do they?

        maybe it's a game
        maybe it's human nature
            see how far
            they can go
            like speeding
            through radar traps

I'm weary of it God
I shake my head
bewildered
    why don't they understand
    there's no free lunch?
will they cheat
to get to heaven?
can they

        help me to be understanding
        to help them
        rather than condemn

        I'm told that's your way

Why Are They So Quick
to Second-Guess Me?

How many times
have we second-guessed you God?
can you count that high?

> you shouldn't have made mosquitos
> or tobacco
> or poisons
> or people for that matter

I know how you feel God
that's the way it is around here
> make a decision
> send out a memo
> change things a bit
> everyone knows better
> what should have been done

why are they so quick
to second-guess me?
why don't they let things
run for a while?
> everyone knows better

> what would you do God
> if you were the boss?
>> er ah
>> I mean
>> what *do* you do
> about second-guessers?
> love 'em
> I guess

My Competitors Are Catching Me!

Ol' Satchel said it first
    I don't look back
    'cause somethin'
    may be gainin' on me

        but I am looking back God
        and Satchel was right
        something *is* gaining on me
          not some thing
          some *one*
          my competitors

God look at all
those competitors
catching me
    the business ones alone
    I could handle
    but suddenly
    they are legion
    and after me
    from all directions

        competitors for my kids
              my wife
           my energies
              my life
          you name it

why do I insist
on running this race alone?
    run side by side
    with me God
    point the way
    help me to see the signposts

the business competitors
I can handle
but while you're at it
you might give me
some help there too

I Wish We Didn't Need Rules

No doubt God
you know that feeling
        you probably said that
        when you gave them
        to Moses
I wish we didn't need rules

                        honor your father
                        remember the Sabbath
                        six days shalt thou labor
                        no other gods

old Israel didn't
do very well
with the rules
much less without them
        so my wish
        is somewhat forlorn
        and pointless

                        without rules indeed
                                sick leave
                                comp time
                                vacation policy
                                insurance forms

thou shalt not kill
thou shalt not steal
thou shalt not covet
not take the name of the Lord

                        it won't work God
                        I wish we didn't need them
                                your rules
                                my rules
                        but we do
                        help us all to see them
                                not as confining
                                but as strengthening
                                as justice

I Wish Everything Were Simple

Ah the good old days
remember them God
when everything was simple?
    you had only
    Adam and Eve
    and the Garden
    unpolluted

I had a simple job
few decisions
nothing ulcer-producing
those were the days
my friend
we thought they'd
never end

but they did

I don't know
when simple went away
and complicated came
to stay

            Adam and Eve
            peopled the earth
            with a vengeance
            I wonder if you anticipated
            Calcutta's poor
            and the Garden
            all the gardens
            lie ravished
            raped by big shovels

it's not simple
for me either God
I didn't anticipate
regulations
and heavy decisions
and production quotas

if it can't be simple any more
for either of us God
let's join hands
you and I
that's something simple we can do

Sometimes I Wish I Were You

I have this image God
of you sitting there
playing chess
    using us as the pieces
    moving
    plotting
    seeing 'way down the line
a master chess player
checkmate!

        and I wish I were you
        sometimes
        not all the time
        just when I need
        to move people
        and scheme things out
        and see
        'way down the line

checkmate!
hah!

        but I suspect
        in my heart of hearts
        that's not how it is
        with you either God

trouble is
you gave us free will
    and I think I know
    how you feel
    when people choose wrong

sometimes I think I am you
    help me to keep it clear
    who I am
    and maybe I won't need
    to be you

I Wish They Wouldn't Try
to Start at the Top

Oh God
no one wants to start
at the bottom
    like I did

        these young ones
        want my job
        now
        as soon as they start
        no patience
        they don't want
        to work up the ladder

      you must know
      how I feel God
      what was it the snake said
      to Eve?

        go ahead eat it
        you will surely not die
        you'll be like God

      right at the beginning
      we all wanted to be
      like you
      or take your place

still and all
it bothers me
they aren't ready for the top
they're green
but they go ahead
and eat of the fruit
they want to be like me
or take my place
now

you've had to deal with us
a long time God
wanting to be you

help me to deal kindly
with them
when they want to start
at the top

It's Tough Being the Boss

I thought it would be fun God
being the boss
    did you?
making deals
making money
making a name

        but it's a headache, God
        it's tough being the boss
        being responsible
        being blamed
        being disliked

    we do the same to you God
    blame you for the weather
    and natural disasters
        hurricanes
        tidal waves
        avalanches
    right there in our insurance policies
    acts of God

when things go wrong here
who gets the blame
the boss, that's who!
    changed the procedures
    tightened the rules
    caused discontent
    acts of boss

        it's tough being the boss
        help me God
        to ride the waves
        on a surfboard

It's Tough Not to Pull Rank

What do you do God
when we don't listen
or when we're too stubborn
to see the good?
  I think I know . . .
  thus says the Lord!
  commands and orders
  thunder down

     it's tough for me Lord
     not to do that
     thus says the boss!
     I want to thunder

     somehow it doesn't work
     as well
     with me

but they won't listen
they're too stubborn
to see the logic
and the benefits

I want to pull rank
forget about persuasion
do it my way
or else
because I'm the boss

     it's habit-forming
     it's tough not to pull rank
     maybe my rank
     isn't all that high

It's Tough to Fire Old Frank

Here I am again God
trying to get enough courage
to fire him
    maybe it isn't courage
    I need
    call it iron guts
    or a cold heart
    I don't know
maybe I shouldn't be boss
if I can't fire him

        what do you do God
        with worn out servants?
        nudge them upstairs?
            is that what you did
            with Elijah
            in the flaming chariot?

he's been loyal
and devoted
but his best days are gone
and there's no chariot
waiting for him

that would be a neat trick though
old Frank would love that
beats a gold watch

        God I think he knows
        he's not pulling his load
        maybe he's expecting
        the ax to fall

I'll call him in
and tell him
    have a good day Frank
    keep up the good work

maybe I need courage
not to fire him

It's Tough To Care — When They Don't

Oh God am I the only one
who cares?
    I know you care Lord
    about people and society
    and suffering and wrongs
but right now I mean
about my business
    I'm not sure
    if you care about that

                I'm not sure anyone does
                besides me
                I see waste all around
                and inefficiency
                and bad work habits
                and no one seems
                bothered by it but me

why should I care Lord
when they don't?
why should I care
about safety and working conditions
better equipment
better lighting
better anything
    why should I care
    when they don't?

                because you care
                that's why
                I knew the answer
                all along

    it's tough to care God
    help me to keep my caring strong

It's Tough Trying To Motivate

God I wish I knew
what Jesus used
to motivate his disciples
    if only I had
    just a little of
    whatever it was

           still they faltered
           and lagged behind
           they stumbled and fell
           and even deserted him
                I know that Lord

still and all
my people need motivation
something from within
    it can't all be
    the promise of rewards
    or some day being the boss
they need something deeper God
having to do with character
    and I doubt I can provide that

        but without that
        it's tough
        trying to motivate them

they don't need skill training
nor additional course offerings
they're too bright as it is
    maybe we need to offer
    character training
    or how to live

    start from scratch it seems

Jesus said
seek first the Kingdom
and then all these things . . .
hmmm
I wonder God
I wonder

It's Tough Telling The Losers

The angels in heaven rejoice . . .
there's hardly anything more enjoyable
than awarding prizes
giving a well deserved promotion
or bonus
placing that laurel wreath
where it surely belongs
      that's when it's fun
      being the boss

            but it's tough
            telling the losers

                  God you know it's tough
                  there were those who didn't make it
                  as Jesus' disciples
                  the laggards
                  the non-committed
                  the losers
maybe Jesus didn't
have to tell them all
      the goats on the left
      the man without the wedding garment
      weeping and gnashing of teeth
      the losers

it's tough telling my people
when they are losers
      they didn't get the promotion
      they didn't have what it takes
      I'll give them a decent recommendation
      there's no good way of saying it

they're losers
and I hurt for them God
I suffer as they turn to walk out
that's when it's not fun
being the boss

Lord, Where Are You?
I'm Hip Deep
In Alligators!

I'm Hip Deep In Alligators!

Why didn't you warn me God
    about this swamp?
    it's full of alligators

        I thought
        getting into this business
        would be a walk in the park
        but I fell into this swamp
    and now they're all around me
    fangs bared
    snapping their jaws
    it's a nightmare God

at first it looked like a dream
so inviting
    a new challenge
    expand my horizons
    move on up
    all those neat sayings

but it's more like a nightmare
I'm fighting for my life, God
this swamp isn't any different
    from the one I left
    why didn't you warn me?

are all swamps full of alligators?
I can't make it alone God
I can't make it alone

The Temptations Are Too Much

Some times God
I can resist everything
except temptation
    and today is one of those times
    and yesterday
    and maybe tomorrow

the temptations are too much
    small temptations
    large temptations
    they come in all sizes
        alter the invoice for a good
        customer
        provide a female companion
            for the visiting big shot
        lie a little to the board
        withhold some facts
        etc

ordinarily God
they might not bother me
too much
but under constant pressure
I often feel like caving in

        I think I know
        how Jesus felt
        when he was tempted
        all the splendor and power
        available
        if only he would bow
        to the offer

so easy to cave in
so difficult to stand firm

help me God
when temptations
look so good
and so harmless
give me strength
to stay on the right path
for its own sake

The Government Is Eating Me Alive

Oh God
the largest alligator of them all
is after me again
I swear God
if you'll pardon me
    the government
      is eating me alive

            I can feel those mighty jaws
            ruthless bureaucratic jaws
            crunching down
            on the business
            slowly
            painfully
            eating me alive

save us God
from our savior government
the inspectors and regulators
the watchers and weighers
the enlighteners who make darkness
the enforcers who make slavery
save us God

            the trouble with this alligator
            is his voracious appetite
            it grows beyond all satisfying
            and it eats us alive

                even vultures
                have the decency
                to wait until death

help me God
as I stand in this swamp
I can't hold off that alligator
much longer
already he's licking his chops

Morally I Was Right But It Hurt Profits

I know I made
the right decision God
    morally I was right
    but it hurt profits
    I can see it already

        I don't know which is worse
        the hurt that goes on inside
        with these decisions
        or the hurting profits
            right now
            both are hurting

what does it profit a man
to gain the whole world
if he loses his soul
Jesus once said
    I'm glad I remembered
    but still it wasn't easy
    it helps God
    if you know how I feel

    why can't my two worlds
    come together
    why is my faith
    always clashing
    with the decisions on my desk?

        will it always be this way?
        was it this way with
        Zacchaeus and Levi
        decisions
        decisions

hurting profits
hurting me
help me God
to walk steady
through the hurts

Help Me, God, To Help Them

Sometimes it's downright scary God
the way they look at me
        my employees
a savior
or benefactor
solver of all problems

            I'm none of these
            but sometimes
            they think I am

            the mantle
            they thrust on me
            is much too big
            for my shoulders

how can I tell them God
        should I tell them
I don't know all the answers
I'm not their guardian angel
        I need more help
than they

                    help me God
                    to help them
                    since I'm the one
                    they turn to

help me God
give me answers
to the unanswerable
insight into complicated problems
strength to aid their weaknesses
and mine

                    stand with me God
                    I can't help them
                    unless you first help me

Where's Solomon — Now That I Need Him?

Where's anybody
when I need them?
old King David
to fight off my enemies
Moses to lead me
out of this wilderness
but right now
I need Solomon
to solve my riddles

I wonder what he'd do
with this sticky one
sometimes I wish
I had lived then
when things were easier

right now I'm dealing with
lives and futures
jobs and households
people making a living
or going broke
and it seems
whichever decision I make
somebody gets hurt

help me God
with the wisdom of Solomon
or the courage of Nathan
the care and concern of Jesus

as I make this decision God
I want it to be the best
not for the sake of my reputation
but for those it will affect
help me God

Help Me, God, to See the Other Side

I know God
there's another side to it
but frankly right now
I don't want to see it
        perhaps deep down
        I'm afraid the other side
        may be as valid
        as my own

                but I spend so much time
                and effort
                building my case
                polishing the arguments
                covering every angle
                I've got a lot invested
                in my side of the story

maybe that's my problem
I hate to see all that effort
go down the drain
or
I hate to lose an argument
maybe that's it

                whatever it is, God,
                help me to
                turn the coin over
                slowly
                cautiously
                to see the other side

the other side
just might be okay
        help me to see it

Let Them Know I Worry Too

I suspect I know
how they picture me
    I remember how
    I once pictured my boss
successful
got it made
somewhat distant and aloof

                the fact is
                I'm swamped with work
                I can't stop and chat
                at every water fountain
                or coffee break

the fact is
I'm swamped with worry
about them
my employees
how can I let them know
I worry about them
I care about them

                I lose sleep
                I lose hair
                I lose my appetite
                worrying and stewing
                about the company
                and all of us

help me to convey that concern
perhaps, God,
if I trusted you more
I wouldn't worry so much
but I still would care
        and I want them
        to know that

To See Your Will in Some of This

God, I often wonder:
are you really here
in the same world
I operate in?
> do you really care
> about production
> and quality control
> and increased sales?
I often wonder

> > where and when
> > do our two worlds meet, God?
> > is yours a Sunday
> > churchy world
> > while mine is buying and selling
> > and meeting and conferring?
> > > do you cross over, God,
> > > into my world
> > > as I do into yours
> > > on Sunday?

> > or are they the
> > same world, God,
> > yours and mine?
> > if so
> > we're in this together
> > what a partnership!

but I need help, God
to see past the graphs and charts
through the quotas and net profits
and the whole nine yards
> I need to see you there
> so the whole thing will
> make more sense
and maybe I'll even discover
your will being done
> in some of this

When I Feel Like Quitting

God, sometimes
I feel like walking out
just quitting the whole thing
    nothing seems to move
    plans go astray
    no one seems to care
    and I too
    want to toss in the sponge

        that's when I need you most, God
        when despair threatens
        and I'm weak enough
        to quit
    give me strength, God
    to rise up
    put one foot forward
    and keep going

quitting isn't like me, God
nor like you
it doesn't fit well
it doesn't taste good
yet sometimes
it's tempting anyway

        it seems to be
        an easy answer
        but it's a non-answer
        it seems an expression
        of freedom
        but may be the bars
        of prison

help me, God,
to overcome that feeling
and to see quitting
for what it is

Leave Some Things in Your Hands

The inclination is
always there God
to do everything myself
    even your job

        it seems so right, God,
        for me to do the things
        others can't do to suit me
        until I find myself
        doing everything

help me, God,
to risk assigning
even the important tasks
to others
    to let them fail occasionally
    to learn by doing
    to enjoy their accomplishments
    as much as I enjoy mine

help me, God,
to trust you enough
to know you'll give them strength
as you do me

        help me, God,
        to leave some things
        in your hands
        to overcome my tendency
        even to look over your shoulder
            to make certain
            you're on the right track

I thanked you God
when I got this job
now let me trust you
without a doubt
to do your part
all by yourself God

Help Me, God, to Be Open to Change

God I thought
it would never happen to me
getting into a rut
resisting change

>   it took me years
>   and sweat and tears
>   to get this business going
>   to get where I am now

>   hurdling problems
>   fighting alligators
>   choosing the right people
>   the right system

and now they
want to change things
the very people I brought up
the bright young heads
and crew I trusted
with our future
ironic
isn't it God?

>   I came in
>   and changed nearly everything
>   and made the wheels turn
>   ironic isn't it?
>   now I resist change
>   I'm almost laughing
>   almost

help me, God,
to be open to new horizons
new people
new ideas and systems
>   in a changing world
>   help me be open
>   to change

*Praise the Lord
For
Molehills!*

The Competition Is Human Too

Lord why do I so often
stand in awe
of the competition
    my knees turn to rubber
    my tongue gets twisted
    I shiver and quake

        they've got perfect records
        they never goof up
        their people are slaves
        they cover the territory
        like a blanket
        fool-proof techniques

    funny I should fear them
    more than I do you at times
    not so funny
    God, what's wrong with me?
    am I less than they?
        I'm afraid to see
        their reports
        do they exaggerate?
        how can they be so great?

        tell me they're human, God
        tell me they're human
        tell me, God, that they foul up
        once in a while

Lord, let me see them
as they are
making a living
    let me see me
    as I am
    making a living
let me see you
as you are
making life

let me be able to shout
confidently
praise the Lord
the competition is human
and praise the Lord
so are you

Praise the Lord For Molehills

Funny thing happened Lord
on the way to
the catastrophe
    someone made a molehill
    out of a mountain

            praise the Lord
            a problem shrank

            it even looked big to me
            at first
            not a mountain maybe
            but no molehill either

praise the Lord
they took down the scaffold
put away the hangman's noose

            I was getting ready
            for a Mt. Everest
            and someone —
            a sainted someone —
            brought it down
            to its intended size
            a molehill
            praise the Lord

I Stood By My Guns

I think I know, Lord,
how the old sheriff felt
in westerns
alone on the dusty street
at high noon

if he was human like me
he was quaking in his boots
I don't consider myself
the hero type
Lord you know my fears
my insecurities

but somehow
praise the Lord
the old adrenalin flowed
when it came high noon last week
and there I was
facing the mob

they seemed to be shooting
from all directions
at the same time

I knew I was right
and I didn't back down
took all they gave
and dealt with it
calm on the outside
sweating blood on the inside

as we left
I think I saw the chairman
wink at me
praise the Lord
I stood by my guns

I Got the Promotion on My Own

I didn't marry
the boss' daughter
I'm not a pal
of the chairman's son

        I don't play golf
        with the biggest customers
        I don't arrange deals
        for the general manager

        praise the Lord
        I got the promotion on my own
        hard work
        doing my job
        and a little bit more
        hustling
        moving
        because I like to accomplish

and I didn't brown-nose
praise the Lord
I didn't brown-nose
I didn't tell the boss
how great he looked
on his 60th birthday
        because he didn't

        maybe I could
        have gotten it earlier
        the promotion
        I don't know

        I've seen some others do it
        sweet talk
        offer themselves
        in any form

                bribe
                purchase
                trade
          thanks but no
          I don't like that route

praise the Lord
I got the promotion
my own way
a way I can live with

Praise the Lord It's Monday

Some say I'm a workaholic Lord
but I don't agree
I just believe
that work is good
and hard work
a form of praise
to you Lord

praise the Lord
for Monday morning
fresh new start
a clean slate
new worlds to conquer
five or six days
full of ripe apples
waiting to be picked

praise the Lord it's Monday
last week's errors are over
can't retrace those steps
time for new beginnings
new hope
new goals
new people

Lord
let my work this week
be a song of joy
a psalm of praise
a dance of thanksgiving

let my accomplishments
be as incense
to you
for giving me work

For Freedom and Opportunity

Praise the Lord
for freedom
    freedom to work
    to earn
    to grow or not to grow
    to climb the mountain
    or walk the valley
freedom

        I returned from Russia
        last week
        on business

        praise the Lord
        for our freedom

        though we've got
        regulations and
        boundaries and
        high taxes and
        a thousand forms to complete
        we still have freedom

and praise the Lord
for opportunity
    always new fields
    reach as far
    as we can see

        develop
        invent
        diversify
        thank God for opportunity

        praise the Lord
        in spite of everything
        and because of you
        it's all worth it

*Blessed Are They
Who Push On
Through
the
Fog*

Blessed Are They
Who Push On Through the Fog

I think I know Lord
I think I have an inkling
what it was like before creation
    fog
    that's what
    misty swirling chaotic fog

        God when you created
        you gave us light
        but around here
        the fog is still so thick
        you could cut it

and bless their hearts
their persevering hearts
those saints of ours
who push on
through the fog

        sometimes I feel, God,
        that Jesus was using me
        as Exhibit A
        the blind leading . . .

whence this fog of ours, God?
misty swirling chaotic fog
    conflicting reports
    confusing orders
    babbling instructions
    undertraining
    over straining
    who's in charge here?
    me

but they like me anyway God
how can I say thanks?
they think the fog will lift soon
and they push on

blessed are they

Blessed Are They Who Bear the Burden
But Don't Need the Honors

Lord some people are built
for receiving honors
they thrive on praise
display their trophies
feed on medals

and then there are
those saints
blessed are they
who also bear the burden
but don't need the honors

blessed are they
who do good work
because it's there
who stay with the problems
'til they win
for the sake alone
of doing it

Lord blessed are they
who scrub the floors
and sort the mail
who clean the conference rooms
and empty the ash trays
where no medals are struck
for the best sweeper

blessed are they
who carry the hidden end
of the company
whose load is just as heavy
but whose names
are unsung
blessed are they
the anonymous heroes

Blessed Are They
Who Know What's Happening

Thanks Lord
for those somewhat scarce
and solid people
who know what's going on

>   no doubt about it, God
>   the maze is confusing
>   even frightening
>   so most people
>   in any company
>   do what they're told
>   but may not know why

the pieces don't easily
fit together
besides we humans
do know how to complicate
even the simplest things
>   we set standards
>   add rule upon rule
>   and make exceptions
>   defer to rank
>   and adopt policies
>   send out instructions

>   and still there are some
>   bless them
>   who know what's happening

unfrightened by the maze
unhurried by the pressure
unconfused by the conflicting orders
>   they pull the ends together
>   and get the job done
>   and carry their department

God bless them
blessed are they
who know what's happening

Blessed Are They
Who Quietly Turn Down a Better Offer

Lord I don't quite know why
he turned down their offer
  it was better pay
  better benefits
  a promotion
maybe it was too good
to be true
I don't know

     but what he said to me was
     "I like working here"
      as simple as that

     I'm not sure
     that's the whole story, God
     but that's what he said
     bless him
     that's what he said

how can you thank people
for loyalty
rewards help
but they won't buy it
it's built in

     blessed are they
     who see green grass
     across the fence every week
     who are beckoned
     and cajoled
     and enticed
     to come on over
   but who stay with us
   make no big deal of it
   don't expect any celebration
   as a result
     blessed are they
     who are loyal

Blessed Are They
Who Do What Couldn't Be Done

Most said it couldn't be done
and frankly
I had my doubts
an outrageous order
a dreamer's deadline
unreality
but some joker
signed the contract
and we were stuck with it
and bless them Lord
they did it
they did what couldn't be done

nobody told them
it couldn't be done
maybe they just
didn't know any better
who knows
but blessed are they
who do the impossible

there are some
in every business
there have to be

they keep the world running
and companies afloat
they keep me sane
and ward off ulcers
those saints

they thrive on problems
even while they fuss

thanks, Lord,
that we have our share
of those who do
what can't be done

Blessed Are They
Who Are Proud of Their Work

Lord you started the trend
in the process of creation
    and God saw
      that it was good
you had good reason, Lord,
to proclaim your work
as being good

             we have not followed suit
             at least not these days
                 most people don't even
                 look at their work
                 to see if it's good

             who cares?

             thanks, God,
             for those who *do* care
             for those rare people
             who enjoy their work
             who are proud
             of what they do
             because it is good

blessed are they
who examine their own work
who strive for excellence
who care about quality
             not for rewards or praise
             but because they are proud —
             proud of being excellent
             in what they do

blessed are they, Lord,
who are their own best critics
who need no inspectors
looking over their shoulders
who leave the job each day
with their heads held high
justly proud
of their work

Blessed Are They Who Love People First

Lord thanks for guys
like Larry
    first rate company
    good products
    and bless him
    a care for people

        the old woman
        he said
        not old enough to retire
        was long past
        carrying her share

        but this was her life
        nothing at home
        this was the only place
        she fit
        so we keep her on
        Larry said
        because she needs it

thanks Lord
for the Larrys of our world
and there are a lot
of them out there

        blessed are they
        who look at the person
        before the product
        who see people
        as your children
        instead of as pawns

blessed are they Lord
who love people first

Blessed Are They
Who Know How To Heal The Hurt

Oh Lord
the hurts do come
at the oddest moments
from unexpected sources
to undeserving servants
an ill chosen word
a misdirected criticism
blame poorly aimed
whatever it is
the hurts do come Lord
one of our worst problems
with work output
worse than sick leave
those hurts
inside the heart
not obvious to most
bottled up
the kind of hurts
workmen's comp doesn't
cover
so both the victim
and the company are losers
and bless them, Lord
we have a few special doctors
not MDs
who know how to heal
their keen eyes and senses
detect the hurt
and unobtrusively
they bring healing
their prescriptions
well chosen words
an attitude of caring
a lift of the spirit
magic potions
blessed are they Lord
who know how to heal the hurt

Blessed Are They
Who Move Up Without Pushing Down

They tell us from the beginning
there's room at the top
you can move on up
there's chance for advancement

> Lord those things
> are so appealing
> who can turn down
> the opportunities to climb?

yet too many
want to win the race
before the starter's gun sounds
or worse yet
trip the other runners

> it saddens me, God,
> when some feel the need
> to push others down
> in order to move up
> it must anger you Lord
> when half truths are used
> in place of competence
> and honest work

God, it's little wonder
we have some bad things
said about us
when you look at the record

> thanks, God,
> for those among us
> who moved up
> through devotion to duty
> honest application of skills
> and good old fashioned
> hard work

blessed are they
who didn't have to
push down
on anybody

Blessed Are They
Who Have Few Regrets

I did
what I had to do
followed through
and said my prayers
what is there to regret?

thanks, God,
for such solid people
people who are not
looking back over their shoulders
doing post mortems
on the irreversible
blessed are they
who have few regrets

God, maybe they can be
an inspiration to the many
who seem to regret
everything they do

if only I had started earlier
or later
if only I had gone to college
or hadn't
or the Marines
or joined my father's firm
etc
regrets regrets
what point is there, Lord?
though we all have
some regrets
for carelessness
or poor judgement
or dumb mistakes at times

help us to know
that what we are doing
is good
that we are going
where we should be
so we can enjoy the trip

blessed are they who lead
in having few regrets

Lord, Will You
Be There
When I
Hang It Up?

Lord Will You Be There
When I Say "We'll Manage — Somehow?"

Lord we've had
some tight tough problems
meeting deadlines
meeting the competition
meeting payroll
    and each time
    somehow we've scraped by
        these people have shown
        enormous trust in me Lord
        so much it scares me
        they believe me
        when I say confidently
        we'll manage
        somehow
    and I don't always know how
    I'm groping in the dark too
        I sweat it out
        watch each crisis pass
        and breathe again
        for another weekend
God I need
that guaranteed loan
of trust and faith
        I can't go on indefinitely
        depending only on my cleverness
        and ability
I need assurance, God,
so when the troops come
with the dark predictions
and notes overdue
I can say
we'll manage
somehow
and be able to smile
knowing you're behind
the promise

Lord Will You Be There
When The Future Looks Shaky?

I've seen it happen Lord
the sunniest picture
framed against a blue sky
suddenly engulfed in storms

I've seen it happen Lord
rosy predictions
the sky's the limit
and suddenly a low hard ceiling

right now we have a sunny picture
a rosy prediction
not a cloud in our sky
vision unlimited
we're on our way

unless
any one or two
of a thousand things
go wrong

and I stand here
almost trembling
in the warm sunshine
and rosy glow
I keep wondering
how long it will last

against that possible
bad weather Lord?
I need a stronger measure
of faith in your promises
particularly that you'll be there
close beside me
when the future looks shaky

Lord Will You Be There
When I Start Looking Over My Shoulder?

Right now Lord
I seem to be running well
confident and strong
ahead of the pack

but I know full well
no one stays in the race
too long

the newer brighter ones
are in the race already
lenthening their strides
making themselves felt
I can't feel their breath yet Lord
but I'm tempted
to look back
over my shoulder
I want to know
how close they're getting

funny thing, Lord
it seems not so long ago
I was entering the race
gaining paces
on the guys in front
I'm not panicky God
not yet
I'm just wondering
since I've never looked back
what it will be like
when I start looking
over my shoulder

and I need to know Lord
that you'll be there
help me to reach back
with the baton
and hand it over gently

Lord Will You Be There
When Our Firm Is Sold?

The rumors are flying
thick and fast, Lord
here at home
or when I travel
there's lots of buzz about it

    Oh God
    I haven't slept well in weeks
      or eaten
      or smiled much

    I think the rumors are true
    they're selling our firm
    and maybe me too
      only
      I might be cashed in
      that's what's gnawing at me

  and it hurts Lord
  deep down it hurts

    all that I've worked for
    the relationships
    the long range plans
    all on the auction block
    it makes me ill Lord

  and it makes me afraid
  afraid they won't need me
  afraid they'll throw out everything
  and start over
    I'm afraid of those high rollers
    and afraid to admit it

Lord will you be there
when our firm is sold?
    erase some of the fear
    ease the pain
    help me to adjust

I need some sleep

Lord Will You Be There
When There Are
No More Mountains To Climb?

Lord with your strength
I've climbed many a mountain
in this business
      scaled perpendicular heights
      crossed treacherous chasms
      escaped the avalanches
      and I know Lord
      a lot of others
      who didn't make it
      to the top

            suddenly it occurs to me God
            all the peaks are below me
            or soon will be

            I can't even imagine it
            I'm getting ready to go again
            and I think
            I've run out of mountains

which way will I turn God?
I can't be president
of the world
I don't want to be

            help me see through the fog, God
            see new horizons
            set new goals
            in case I need
            to change directions

            Lord be there
            when there are
            no more mountains to climb

Lord Will You Be There
When I Hang It Up?

We're strange creatures God
we humans
when we're giving it all we've got
long hours
long weeks
we make lots of noise
about wanting to retire
      it's easy to say that
      when it's much too early

         but now Lord
         it isn't so early any more
         and those retirement wishes
         will soon come back
         to haunt me

I'm not too concerned
what I'll do God
      secretly I'm worried
      about the company

         somehow Lord
         it doesn't feel good
         to imagine that
         things will go on just fine
         without me

will they miss me, God?
will they wish I were back
in harness again?
should I call in to check up
or just to say hello?

         I'm not there yet, God
         but it's close down the road
         and
         I'm going to need you
         more than ever
         when I hang it up